This Book Belongs To:

Made in the USA
Middletown, DE
21 June 2022

67522572R00068